Las Vegas Hiking Guide

Paula M. Jacoby-Garrett

Traveling Books & Maps
4001 S. Decatur #34
Las Vegas, NV. 89103

ZING PUBLISHING

Copyright ©1997 by Zing Publishing

All rights reserved, no part of this book may be reproduced without written permission, except for the inclusion of brief quotations in a review. The author/publisher assume no liability, the use of this book indicates the assumption and responsibility of risk.

Published and Distributed by:
Zing Publishing
1306 W. Craig Road, Suite E, #103
North Las Vegas, NV 89030

ISBN 0-9658439-0-4

Printed on recycled paper.

Cover Photo: Red Rock Canyon
Back Cover Photos (clockwise):
    Kathy Joy at Lovell Canyon
    Eileen and Paul Bengtson at Cave Trail
    Bill, Paula and Jaz Garrett at Bonanza Trail
    Sylvia Jacoby at Wetlands Trail
    Dave Vozka at Railroad Trail

All photos by the author except Bonanza Trail photo on back cover by George Jacoby.

Dedication

This book is dedicated to the memory of E. Lorraine Putnam. She was a friend, colleague and hiking partner. Her love and wonder of nature and the outdoors was an inspiration. She is deeply missed.

Table of Contents

Introduction 1
Las Vegas Map & Getting Around 5
Red Rock Canyon 7
    Calico Hills 9
    Calico Tanks 10
    Cave Trail 11
    Children's Discovery Trail 12
    Ice Box Canyon 13
    Keystone 14
    La Madre Spring 15
    Lost Creek 17
    Moenkopi 18
    Oak Creek Canyon 19
    Pine Creek Canyon 21
    Turtlehead Peak 23
    White Rock Spring 24
    Willow Spring 25
Mount Charleston 27
    Bonanza Trail 29
    Bristlecone 32
    Cathedral Rock 34
    Charleston Peak Trail 35
    Fletcher Canyon 38
    Little Falls Spring 39
    Mary Jane Falls 40
    Muddy Springs 41
    Mummy Springs 43

    Robber's Roost 45

    Trail Canyon 46

Sheep Mountains 47

    Hidden Forest 49

    Joe May Canyon 50

Valley of Fire 53

    Clark's Wash 55

    Petroglyph Canyon 56

    White Dome Loop 58

Lake Mead 59

    Bowl of Fire 61

    Callville 64

    Goldstrike Canyon 65

    Grapevine Canyon 67

    Historic Railroad Trail 69

    Horsethief Canyon 71

    Lovell Wash 73

    Northshore Summit 75

    Redstone 75

    River Mountain Trail 77

    Roger's Spring 79

    Wetlands Trail 80

    White Rock Canyon 81

Keyhole Canyon 83

Top 10 Hikes 85

Parents with Children 86

Special Thanks 87

Introduction

This hiking book is for the Las Vegas and surrounding area. A general description, difficulty, seasonal preference and length are given for each hike and will assist you in determining which hike(s) best suit your interests and physical aptitude. The key to an enjoyable hiking experience is to prepare yourself and hike within your physical means. Below is a sampling of what you may need, and may encounter on any given hike as well as precautions you can take to maintain your safety and health.

The proper outfitting.

Sun screen. A high SPF rating such as 25 is best. Using the waterproof type helps to maintain coverage while sweating.

Water or sports drink. Not soda, not iced tea, not beer, but WATER or SPORTS DRINK. In the dry climate of the Southwest it is very easy to become dehydrated so drink up. The amount your body needs varies from person to person. I suggest taking water in liter quantities, none of those little 8oz. bottled water containers, but at least one liter no matter how short the hike. I often take two liters for myself in the summer months, for an easy to moderate hike. To keep water cool, you can freeze a container half, to three quarters full of water overnight, and add the remainder in the morning before the hike.

First aid kit. For shorter hikes I often leave it in the car, and for longer hikes take it with me. Kits are available commercially or can be pieced together from household stocks.

Shoes. Whether it's hiking boots, tennis shoes or sport sandals, a good tread is the key. For the best support and protection, hiking boots are the first choice.

Clothes. A wide brimmed hat and sunglasses will protect from the sun. For those sensitive to the sun, a little more protection may be needed; wear a long sleeved cotton shirt with loose fitting slacks.

Tweezers. My dogs and I have, on numerous occasions, found ourselves with cactus spines imbedded in our bodies. It is much more pleasant to remove them immediately than wait for the long walk back to the car and drive home.

Precautions.

Never trust a friendly snake. The desert is a harsh place. Animals and plants bite, poke, sting and hide to protect themselves. The best protection from such creatures is to be knowledgeable about them. For example, rattlesnakes. Everyone that comes to visit from other areas of the country are concerned about them. "There won't be any rattlesnakes, will there?" With all the hiking I do in this area I rarely see rattlesnakes. So relax. If you do see or hear such a creature move in the opposite direction, slowly.

Every arroyo was a wild river in a former day. Washes are great fun to hike in and you can frequently get some shade. But washes are also deadly killers. I am more concerned about being caught in a deep wash during a rainstorm than any snake or scorpion the desert has to offer. A rain cloud in the distance can send a wall of water at you even if it isn't raining in your immediate vicinity. The water moves so quickly and unexpectedly that there is no time to react. The best way to avoid such an occurrence is to watch the weather reports and be aware of potential storming in the surrounding areas.

A heap of mistakes adds up to a little experience. Everyone makes mistakes at some time or another and hiking is not exempt from that. In fact, exchanging stupid hiking tales is a common way that hikers learn from each other. One of the most important things I have learned is the importance of telling someone of your hiking plans. Yes, it is fun to be spontaneous, but hiking can be dangerous and it should be given adequate respect. What *I* do, is call someone, tell them of my hiking plans (where and when) and give them a time deadline. If I am not back at that time, that person is to call the appropriate authorities. It may be inconvenient but it could be a life saver.

Trail Etiquette

- The desert is a fragile environment and reproduces slowly, so stay on the trail.
- Those traveling uphill have the right of way. Stop, move to the side and let them pass.
- Don't litter.
- If you hike with your dog, be considerate of others. If your pet defecates on the trail, remove it from the trail.
- Many of these hikes have historic features which are protected by law. Leave these structures and artifacts in place.
- Pack out all human waste and toilet paper (use sealable plastic bags). If this is not possible, bury the waste a minimum of six inches in depth.

Terms

hiking - walking in natural surroundings, may be strenuous dependant on the terrain.

backpacking - an overnight hiking trip where one carries a backpack with camping gear.

rock scrambling - moving over rocks using hands and feet

arroyo-a wash or drainage in which water flows after a rain

Maps

If you want more information about an area, a U.S. Geological Survey (USGS) map is the best choice. For several of the longer hikes in this book, the USGS map that correlates with that hike is listed. These maps are handy when exploring an area or attempting a more complicated or lengthy hike. The best places to find these maps in this area are:

Traveling Books & Maps
4001 S. Decatur #34
Las Vegas, NV 89103
(702) 871-8082 or Out of State 1-800-240-1774

Mercury Blueprint & Supply Co., Inc.
2910 S. Highland Dr., Ste. H
Las Vegas, NV 89109
(702) 794-4400

Please Note: All distances described for length or elevation in this book are approximate.

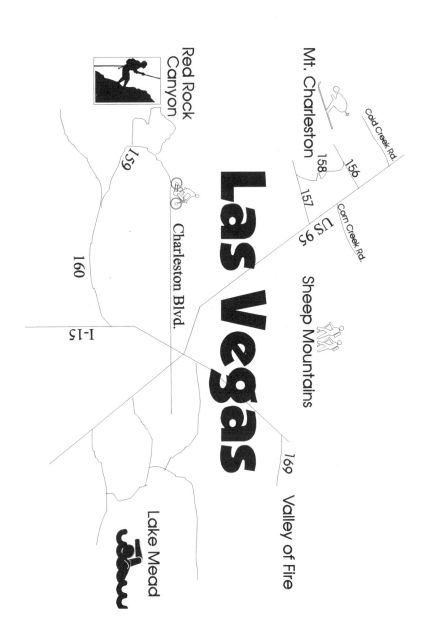

Getting Around

There are 5 major areas covered in this book; Red Rocks, Mt. Charleston, Sheep Mountains, Valley of Fire, and Lake Mead. Red Rocks can be reached by taking Charleston Blvd. west or taking Blue Diamond Road (160) to State Route 159 west.

To get to Mt. Charleston, take US 95 north out of town. Depending on the area you are hiking, take Route 157 towards Kyle Canyon, or continue on US 95 to Route 156 towards Lee Canyon. Cold Creek is north of the Lee Canyon turnoff on US 95 to the left on Cold Creek Road (there is a correctional facility on the corner).

The hikes described on the Sheep Mountains are reached from US 95 north from Las Vegas to the Corn Creek turnoff (17 miles past Craig road). The turnoff is indicated by a sign for the Desert National Wildlife Range.

Valley of Fire is located northeast of Las Vegas. It can be reached via Lake Mead's Northshore Road which is scenic but a slow route. The faster alternative is to take I-15 north from Las Vegas to the 169 turnoff and drive east to the park.

Lake Mead and the hikes in the area cover a wide region. Generally, the lake can be accessed over Sunrise Mountain via Lake Mead Blvd. on the northeast side of the city, via Lake Mead Drive on the southeast side of the city, or from Boulder City. More specific directions are given on the individual hike description text in the following pages.

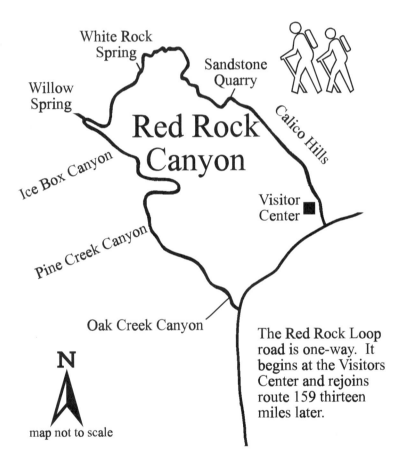

Red Rock Canyon National Conservation Area

Managed by the Bureau of Land Management

For more information contact:
Red Rock Canyon Visitor Center
(702) 363-1921

There will soon be a fee (not yet enacted at time of printing) for entering the Red Rock Canyon Loop Road. The fees are on a daily basis, or a year pass can be obtained.

A variety of books and pamphlets are available at the Visitor Center about the desert, Las Vegas and the Red Rock Canyon area. One in particular is the **Red Rock Canyon Trail Guide** which is a "must have" for any hiker. It is extremely reasonably priced and gives a lot of information not only about the hikes at Red Rock, but the vegetation and wildlife too.

Calico Hills

General Description: Various trails leading through spectacular sandstone formations.

Difficulty: Easy to Difficult (terrain near the parking lots are level or slightly hilly, the further into the hills you go the more difficult the hiking.)

Best Time of Year to hike: Fall through Spring

Length: Variable

Directions: Drive to Red Rock Canyon National Conservation Area (see map and directions on p.5). At the stop sign continue straight into the park. Take the first or second pullout on your right and park.

Hike: Trails lead from the parking area in various directions. This is a good area to hike the distance and the level you feel comfortable. Spectacular views of the sandstone formations are visible from the parking lot, or you can hike among them. Remember rock scrambling and climbing can be dangerous so take caution and hike within your limits. It is very easy to get lost among these formations so hike accordingly. Many rock climbers use this area, so you may get a glimpse of them in action.

Calico Tanks

General Description: A hike to a large, shallow rock depression where water may be present.

Difficulty: Moderate (elevation gain, some rock scrambling)

Best Time of Year to hike: Fall through spring

Length: 1.2 miles one-way

Elevation: 4500 ft to 4900 ft

Directions: Drive to Red Rock Canyon National Conservation Area (see map and directions on p. 5). At the stop sign continue straight into the park. Approximately 2.6 miles from the stop sign is the turnoff to Sandstone Quarry. Turn right and park in the parking area.

Hike: The trail-head begins at the Sandstone Quarry parking area. A short walk along a closed dirt road will take you to large cut boulders from the active period of the quarry. Cross the wash to the left. After 0.2 mile the trail will fork, stay to the right. Follow the trail as it leads to a canyon with red sandstone on your left and white on your right. The trail is often difficult due to many side trails leading off in all directions, just keep working your way up the canyon. As you proceed up in elevation, you will be lead to a narrow outlet beyond which is the Calico Tank. If you continue along the right side of the tank you will gain a worthwhile view of the Red Rock valley and of Calico Basin.

Cave Trail

General Description: An interesting day hike up a canyon to a cave system.

Difficulty: Easy (rock scrambling at the very end of the hike to the cave entrance)

Best Time of Year to hike: Fall through Spring

Length: 1.0 mile one-way

Directions: Take Charleston Blvd. west towards Red Rock Canyon. Turn left and park in a dirt parking area 0.85 mile past the entrance to Red Rock Canyon.

Hike: Also called the Hippy Caves, the caves of this area have been used for years by the people of Las Vegas. The trail begins on the east side of the parking area, leading you from the parking area on flat level ground, and becomes increasingly steep as you move up the canyon. The first part of the hike you will be on the south side of the canyon, then the trail winds across the canyon to the north side. The caves are at the trail end, just as you cross the canyon. You will need to scan the hillside to find the entrance, some spray painting on boulders will help you find it. Remember caves can be very dangerous so do not enter them unless you have training and expertise in caving.

Children's Discovery Trail

General Description: A short interactive desert hike ranging from open desert to hillside.

Difficulty: Easy

Best Time of Year to hike: Fall through Spring

Length: 1.0 mile loop

Directions: Drive to Red Rock Canyon National Conservation Area (see map and directions on p. 5). At the stop sign continue straight into the park. Continue for 7.5 miles until reaching the Willow Spring turnoff on your right. Park at a pullout on the left (0.2 miles from the loop road).

Hike: Stop at the visitor's center before starting this hike for the Children's Discovery Trail Guide. It's free, but you have to ask for it at the information counter. The trail has marked stopping points where the children can refer to their guide to learn interesting facts about the area.

The hike begins at a well marked trail head and information board. It starts in open desert, crosses a large wash, then begins to climb the hillside. After 0.25 mile the trail will junction with the Willow Spring Loop Trail. After 0.36 mile the trail joins the Lost Creek Trail and from that point descends down the hillside to the parking area.

Ice Box Canyon

General Description: A rock scrambling hike to a dry waterfall.

Difficulty: Moderate (rock scrambling)

Best Time of Year to hike: Fall through Spring

Length: 1.15 miles one-way

Directions: Drive to Red Rock Canyon National Conservation Area (see map and directions on p. 5). At the stop sign continue straight into the park. Continue just short of 8 miles until reaching the Ice Box Canyon parking area.

Hike: The hike begins at the parking lot. Follow the obvious trail across a large wash. The trail continues across desert and begins following the north side of Ice Box canyon. After some distance the trail drops down into the canyon. Don't be worried about missing the turn into the canyon, if you continue on the rim, the trail ends abruptly at a large impassible rock formation. Turn around and return the way you came until you reach the trail turnoff.

Once entering the canyon, the trail becomes obscure. Keep following the wash up the canyon. Large boulders in several areas limit access up the canyon, this is where rock scrambling is needed. The trail ends at a seasonable waterfall. Return the way you came.

Keystone

General Description: A hike through the desert to a small canyon and if desired, up a ridge for a extraordinary view of the area.

Difficulty: Easy (more difficult to the scenic overlook)

Best Time of Year to hike: Fall through Spring

Length: 1 mile one-way

Directions: Drive to Red Rock Canyon National Conservation Area (see map on p. 5). At the stop sign continue straight into the park. Just shy of 6 miles turn right into the White Rock Spring area. Drive to the turn around and park.

Hike: This trail moves from old dirt road to trail and back to dirt road so watch signs and landmarks carefully. Start the hike to the right side of the dirt turn around at an obvious trail. There will be a sign indicating the direction of the trail after a short distance. This trail will join with a road, hike uphill to the left.

As you level out there will be a large ridge called Hogback Ridge on your right. A small trail to your right leads up the ridge for a tremendous view of the area. This trail is obvious at first then is almost impossible to follow. Just hike uphill to the top for the view.

If you continue on the main trail, the road will fork just beyond the ridge. Take the trail to the right that leads downhill into an open area and canyon. Just shy of 0.20 of a mile down the hill is a large ravine, an excellent spot to picnic or a terror of a spot if you have small children. Return the way you came.

La Madre Spring

General Description: A hike up through hilly upper desert to a dammed spring.

Difficulty: Easy to the dam
          Moderate to the spring (rock scrambling)

Best Time of Year to hike: Fall through Spring

Length: 1.5 miles one-way

Directions: Drive to Red Rock Canyon National Conservation Area (see map and directions on p. 5). At the stop sign continue straight into the park. Continue for 7.5 miles to the Willow Spring turnoff. After 0.6 mile the pavement will end. If you do not have high clearance vehicle, park here and walk up the road just over a 0.5 mile to the La Madre trail-head (the hike would then be 4.0 miles round trip). If you drive on the dirt portion you will find several pullout areas to park on the side of the road. There is a sign marking the trail-head that is clearly visible from the road.

Hike: Begin the hike at the trail-head. The hike follows an old road to the dam making this portion of the hike quite easy. Stay on the main trail ignoring a few paths and an old road that branch off to the right into the large wash area. Shortly before the dam, the road appears to fork then join again. In this area there are two building foundations from years past. The hike continues on the trail up a hill to the dam. This is a great area to picnic and relax.

For those wanting to hike further, the stream continues up the canyon. The hiking becomes more challenging with a narrower path and on occasion crossing the stream and mild rock scrambling. This is a great area to do some exploring; the canyon forks a few times and with the abundant water there are sure to be lots of interesting wildlife in the area. Keeping along the main streambed you will find the trail is somewhat vague at times. At one point the trail is along the left ridge above the stream then dips down into the stream, here there are wild grapevines abounding. This is about 0.25 mile from the dam. Return the way you came.

Lost Creek

General Description: A short fun hike to a box canyon with a seasonal waterfall.

Difficulty: Easy

Best Time of Year to hike: Fall through Spring

Length: 0.3 mile one-way

Directions: Drive to Red Rock Canyon National Conservation Area (see map and directions on p. 5). At the stop sign continue straight into the park. Continue for 7.5 miles until reaching the Willow Spring turnoff on your right. Park at a pullout on the left (after 0.2 miles).

Hike: The hike begins at a clearly marked trail-head and information board. Walk along the trail in a level open desert area, across a large wash and up the hillside. The trail will become narrower with some side trails evident. Lush vegetation followed by large boulders keep the hike  twisted and interesting. Along the way there is a small stream on the left, at one point there is park benches near the stream which makes a wonderful resting spot. The trail ends at a box canyon. Seasonally there is a waterfall. The high canyon walls and mature vegetation make the end of this trail a nice picnic spot.

Moenkopi

General Description: A short hike up and down hills and along small ridges.

Difficulty: Easy

Best Time of Year to hike: Fall through Spring

Length: 2.0 mile loop

Directions: Drive to Red Rock Canyon National Conservation Area (see map and directions on p. 5). At the stop sign turn left to the Visitor Center. Park in the parking lot. The trail begins on the left (south side) of the Visitor Center.

Hike: The hike begins at a marked trail-head. Throughout this hike other trails join and leave from the Moenkopi trail so watch marked posts at each junction. This trail loops around the desert around the Visitor Center giving a hiker great views of the Red Rock area. The trail goes in and out of washes, up on ridges from the north to the south and then east, back to the Visitor Center.

Oak Creek Canyon

General Description: A scenic hike up a canyon to a stream.
Difficulty: Easy to the canyon
             Moderate in the canyon (rock scrambling)
Best Time of Year to hike: Fall through Spring
Length: 1.10 one-way to the canyon (various up the canyon)
Directions: Drive to Red Rock Canyon National Conservation Area (see map and directions on p. 5). At the stop sign continue straight into the park. The Oak Creek turnoff is the last dirt road on you right on the thirteen mile loop road. Drive down the dirt road to a circular parking area at the end.

Hike: This hike is described from the Oak Creek parking area off the loop road of Red Rock Canyon. From the parking area follow the obvious trail near the information boards. The trail begins across open desert. As you near the canyon from the north side you will notice a large hill on the south side of the canyon. This is known as Potato Knoll. There is a side trail that takes you to the base of the knoll and around the back side.

The main trail, however, continues along the side of the canyon and then drops into the canyon after 1.10 mile. The one difficulty of this hike is there are trails everywhere and it is easy to get confused on which trail to take. The general idea is to hike from the parking area along the north side, then drop down into the canyon, then hike up canyon. There are trails that will take you into the canyon sooner, there are trails that will hug the north side then drop down into the canyon,

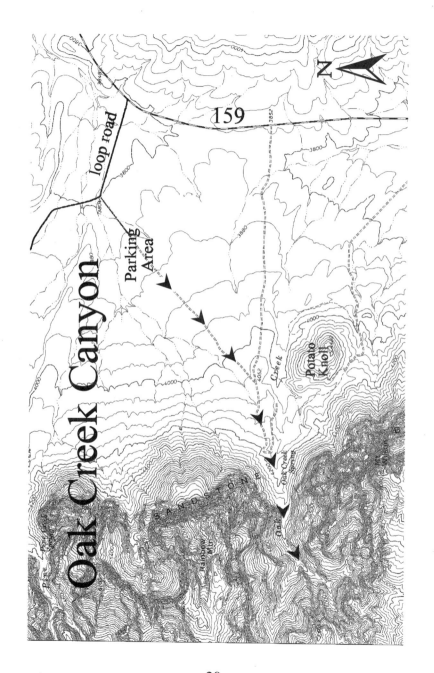

either way, up the canyon is the key. If you were looking for an easy hike, stop at the canyon and enjoy the view then return the way you came. If you are ready for some serious rock scrambling, continue up stream.

Water levels in the canyon will vary seasonally. It is common to find small waterfalls and pools as you hike up the canyon. There is so much fun rock scrambling to be had up stream, continue as fall as your abilities will take you.

Generally speaking as you near a fork in the canyon, the trail becomes even more difficult. The preferred route is to continue up the canyon on the left fork. Return the way you came.

Pine Creek Canyon

General Description: A fun hike up a pine filled canyon.
Difficulty: Easy to homestead
Moderate up canyon (rock scrambling)
Best Time of Year to hike: Fall through Spring
Length: 0.75 miles one-way to homestead
various if hiking up the canyon
Directions: Drive to Red Rock Canyon National Conservation Area (see map and directions on p. 5). At the stop sign continue straight into the park. After 10 miles park in the Pine Creek Canyon parking area on your right.
Hike: Begin at the marked trail-head in the parking area. The trail drops from the parking area, continues across the desert then parallels the canyon.

The trail is very well maintained to the homestead. What's left of the homestead is a foundation. It will be on your left as you hike on the trail so keep a watchful eye or you may miss it.

Continuing beyond the homestead the trail starts nicely and goes quickly downhill (of course this is half the fun!). After you've been on the trail for about a mile the trail will appear to cross the stream. It is better to keep on the right side of the canyon (north).

From here on in it is a bush wacking, rock scrambling adventure. Follow what little trail is there, if it doesn't seem right follow the stream bed. The canyon does fork a couple times; take the south fork the first time it splits and the north fork the second time. This is the 'preferred' route but hiking is for the adventure so do what you please. Return the way you came.

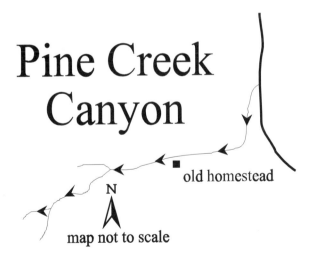

Turtlehead Peak

General Description: A challenging hike up to a spectacular 360°view.

Difficulty: Difficult (elevation gain and loose footing)

Best Time of Year to hike: Fall through Spring

Length: 2.5 miles one-way

Elevation: 4500 ft to 6323 ft

Directions: Drive to Red Rock Canyon National Conservation Area (see map and directions on p. 5). At the stop sign continue straight into the park. Approximately 2.6 miles from the stop sign turn right at the Sandstone Quarry turnoff. Park in the parking area near the restrooms.

Hike: The hike begins at a clearly marked trail-head and information board near the restrooms. Look up, above the pale sandstone. That large dark grey peak behind the sandstone is Turtlehead (it looks quite impressive from the parking lot). Follow the trail to an open area with large cut boulders in front of you. Continue on the trail to the left of the boulders as it crosses a large wash. After 0.2 miles you will reach a fork in the trail, stay to the left.

From here, the trail moves up along hilltops, down into washes again and again. The general idea is to go around a large section of light colored sandstone on the northwestern side (left). The trail becomes obscure in several places so keep watch. As you round the side of the sandstone you will cut between two sections then wander up towards the peak.

Watch for rock cairns along the trail indicating the way. The trail goes up the hillside in a large drainage system on the western (left) side of the peak, then across a ridge to the peak. After 1.2 miles you reach the first of the rock scrambling areas up the trail. If a section seems too difficult, look around, there are often alternatives up a difficult area. It may seem favorable to forgo the rock cairns and take a short cut more directly towards the peak. Don't do it. The best trail is the marked trail, it directs the easiest and safest course.

When you reach the ridge line, follow it to the east towards the peak, then to the south and the top of the peak. The top is spectacular with 360° views. Return the way you came and watch your footing, the trail has lots of loose rocks.

White Rock Spring

General Description: A hike to a water catchment.
Difficulty: Easy
Best Time of Year to hike: Year-round
Length: 0.3 mile one-way
Directions: Drive to Red Rock Canyon National Conservation Area (see map and directions on p. 5). At the stop sign continue into the park for 5.8 miles until you reach the White Rock Spring pull off. Turn right and park in the parking area.
Hike: The trail-head begins on the left side of the dirt turn around. The trail is a closed dirt road that descends to the spring and water catchment. Manmade water catchments like this one help extend the range of wildlife by providing a year-round water source. Return the way you came.

Willow Spring Loop

General Description: A pleasant hike in the Willow Spring area of Red Rocks.

Difficulty: Easy

Best Time of Year to hike: Fall through Spring

Length: 1.2 mile loop

Directions: Drive to Red Rock Canyon National Conservation Area (see map and directions on p. 5). At the stop sign continue into the park for 7.5 miles until reaching the Willow Spring turnoff on your right. Park at the first pullout on the left (after 0.2 miles) or at the picnic area at the end of the paved road.

Hike: This hike can begin in several different ways. The hike described here is starting from the Lost Creek parking area and beginning the hike in an easterly direction.

From the parking area, cross the road at the crosswalk and follow the obvious trail. The trail will lead up the hill and to the left. Continue on this trail until reaching the picnic area. The trail will be paved for a short distance then the paved portion of the trail turns left, continue straight. The trail runs along large boulders to the right. At this point the trail becomes obscure, make your way left through the picnic area to the road. The trail continues across the road with a small trail sign and obvious trail. Shortly the trail crosses a large wash and continues up a hillside. About 0.35 from the picnic area the trail will junction with the Children's Discovery Trail. You can turn left or right, either way is about the same distance to the end point. The right trail is more interesting with a short hike across the hillside meeting with the Lost Creek Loop after about a 0.1 mile. At this point there is a small stream with lots of shade that runs along the trail which makes a good respite. Continue to the left down the hill to the parking area.

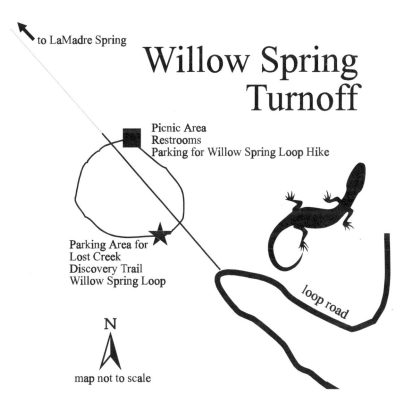

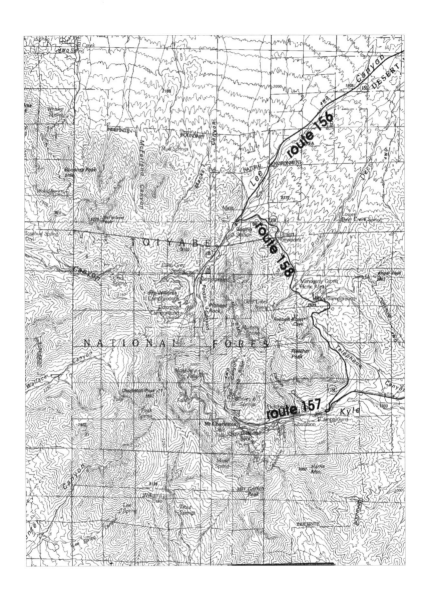

Mount Charleston

Managed by the U.S. Forest Service

For More Information contact:

Toiyabe National Forest
Las Vegas Ranger District
2881 S. Valley View
Suite # 16
Las Vegas, NV 89102
(702)873-8800

The Kyle Canyon Ranger Station is a great source for information (off Route 157, past the Route 158 turnoff, on the left side of the road). There are several pamphlets about hiking and camping in the area, as well as Forest Service personnel that are there to answer questions.

Bonanza Trail

General Description: A challenging hike from Lee Canyon across the mountain range to the Cold Creek area.

Difficulty: Difficult   (length, elevation gain, high altitude)

Best time of Year to Hike: Spring through fall.

Length: 15 miles using the Bristlecone southwest trail
                16 miles using the Bristlecone northeast trail

Elevation: 8630' at Bristlecone parking area to 7550' at Bonanza parking area, with the highest elevation on the trail being approximately 10,300'.

USGS map: Charleston Peak, Cold Creek, Wheeler Well

Directions: Take U.S. 95 north to Route 156. Turn left toward Lee Canyon. After 16.7 miles, turn right (shortly before McWilliams campground) onto a short dirt road ending at a dirt parking area. Park there for the northeast Bristlecone approach or at the ski area parking lot for the southwest approach.

Hike: This hike can be done either as a day hike or a backpacking trip. Doing it as a day-hike is pleasant because you don't have to carry so much equipment, but if you are looking for a night away from civilization, try it as a backpacking trip. Either way, the trail provides spectacular views and since this trail is not in heavy use, solitude. I would suggest looking at the USGS maps for this area before hiking.

The hike can be attempted from either direction, from Lee Canyon to the Cold Creek area or the opposite. The hike described here is from Lee Canyon. Since this is not a loop hike, have a car awaiting you on the opposite end.

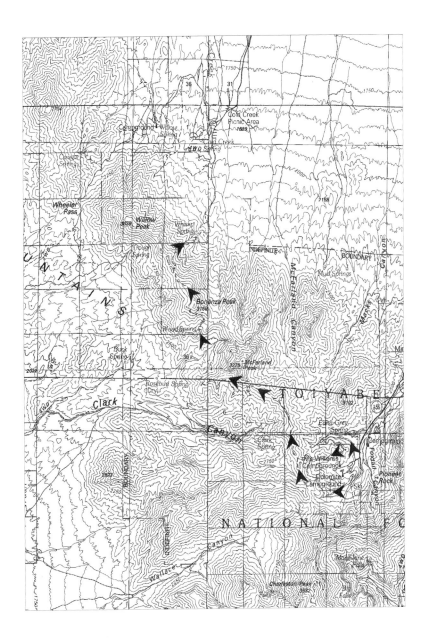

When deciding between the southwest and northeast approach from the Bristlecone trail note that the southwest approach although a mile shorter is a bit more difficult. The northeast trail is a former road so elevation change is very gradual Either way you choose, follow the trail until meeting up with the Bonanza trail-head. From there the trail will rise in elevation through a series of switchbacks until reaching the ridge line. At this point there is a fork in the trail, continue to the right.

The trail continues for several miles along a ridge line offering excellent viewing but also providing some risk due to weather. Make certain to watch weather reports before hiking, and keep an eye out for storms while on the trail.

Just before getting to McFarland peak you reach a spectacular saddle with breathtaking views to the east and west.

At McFarland peak, the trail begins to wind around to the west, working toward Bonanza peak. There is a very small spring along the trail, in the valley before reaching Bonanza peak. This is a good area for camping, in fact, if you look to the northwest of the spring you will see a teepee frame. At that spot there is a good camping area with level ground.

From the spring, follow a series of switchbacks up the mountain. The trail doesn't actually go to the peak's highest point but on the trail there is a rock formation with arrows pointing the way if you want to reach the top of the peak.

The trail continues to follow the west side of the peak in a northernly direction, eventually winding around to a series of switchbacks, down to the parking area south of Cold Creek.

Bristlecone Trail

General Description: A loop trail with spectacular views, through the forests of Mt. Charleston.

Difficulty: Moderate   (elevation change)

Best Time of Year to hike: Spring through fall

Length: 6.15 mile loop

Elevation: 8629', to 9400' at the highest point

USGS map: Charleston Peak

Directions: Take US 95 past Route 157 to Route 156. Turn left and follow the road for 16.7 miles until reaching a gravel road on your right. Park in the obvious parking lot. If you reach the McWilliams campground you have gone a bit too far.

Hike: This is a great hike to take when the aspens are changing color in fall. The trail-head begins as a closed gravel road just beyond the parking area. Follow the trail as it initially heads to the north, then west, and for the last leg of the trail to the east. The trail will wind upward into the forest giving spectacular views of the mountains. Throughout the hike, the trail moves in and out of small ravines thereby giving occasional elevation gain and loss. The end of the trail is the upper parking area for Lee Canyon Ski Area. Follow the road down the hill until reaching the gravel road and your vehicle. This hike can also be completed in reverse; starting at the ski area and finishing at the gravel parking area. It makes no difference but you may want to think of the hike up the hill to the ski resort in planning.

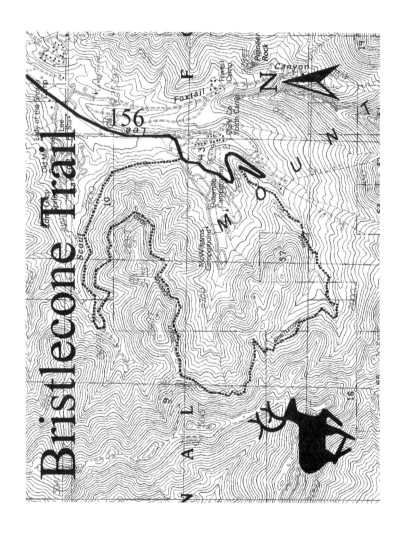

Cathedral Rock

General Description: A short day-hike to the best views of Kyle Canyon.

Difficulty: Moderate (elevation change)

Best Time of Year to hike: Spring through Fall

Length: 1.4 miles one way

Elevation: 7645' at the parking area and 8,600' at the peak

Directions: Take route 95 north to Route 157 (7.5 miles past Craig Road). Travel west on Route 157 for 20 miles until you reach the parking area which is the first established parking area on your right after the extreme turn and ascent of highway 157.

Hike: The trail-head begins at the parking area up the embankment (there is a restroom near the steps). Follow the trail to the left. The trail winds through pine and aspen and to a series of switchbacks. A quarter mile from the summit, or 1.15 from the beginning of the hike, the trail splits. There will be a large path on the left at a slightly higher level, and a narrow path below. Take the narrow path on your right to a series of small switchbacks leading to the top of the peak. The summit has magnificent views and is a good place to sit awhile and take in all that surrounds you. Be careful of the extreme drop off in the area, keeping a close watch on children and pets. Return the way you came.

Charleston Peak Trail

General Description: A challenging hike up to the Charleston Peak at 11,900 feet.

Difficulty: Difficult (elevation change, high altitude, length)

Best Time of Year to hike: late Spring through early Fall

Length: 10 miles one-way using the North Loop Trail
8 miles one-say using the South Loop Trail
18 miles using both trails as a loop

Elevation: 7,810' at the trail-head, 11,915' at the highest point

USGS maps: Charleston Peak, Griffith Peak

Directions: Take route 95 north to Route 157 (7.5 miles past Craig Road). Travel west on Route 157 for 20.4 miles until you reach an extreme turn in the road. Continue straight onto Echo Road until reaching extreme u-turn. Park on the left.

Hike: This is a very difficult hike for several reasons. One is the altitude. Most of us don't live at high altitude so we are at a disadvantage when attempting this hike. One common problem of high altitude is altitude sickness. It starts with a loss of appetite, then headache, weakness, possibly progressing to dizziness and nausea. The best way to prevent this is to take it slow. Breathe fully, take long rests and drink lots of water.

Which brings me to the next point, water. This hike can be accomplished in two different ways; as a backpacking trip or as a day hike. Backpacking seems the obvious because you don't have to go as far in one day, but not only must you carry all your backpacking gear, but lots of water. There is not water available on the trail so you must pack your own. The

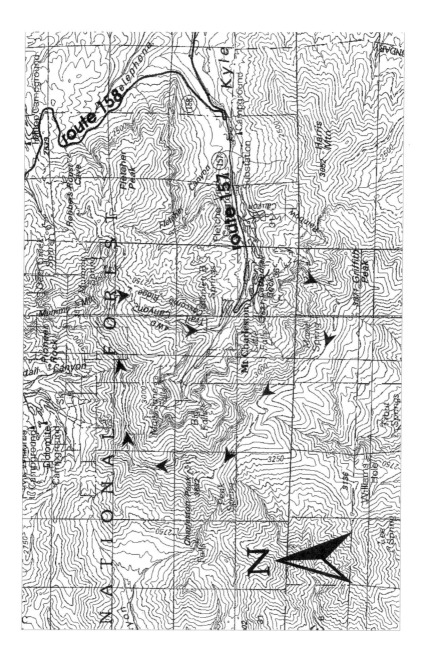

choice is yours but don't short change yourself and not bring enough water.

The hike is in Kyle Canyon and begins from either the Trail Canyon (North Loop), or Cathedral Rock (South Loop) trail-head. I would suggest looking at the USGS map for this area before hiking. The entire loop can be hiked or just the South trail or just the North trail. The entire loop trail will be described here. To cut some of the distance, one alternative is to have two vehicles, one at the Trail Canyon trail-head, the other at the South Loop/Cathedral Rock trail-head.

Begin at the Trail Canyon trail-head off Echo Road. After 2.0 miles the trail will join with the North Loop trail. Follow the trail to the left (west). You will know you are close to the peak when you start switchbacks up to Charleston Peak.

For part of this hike, the trail is exposed. Watch weather reports before hiking and take note while on the trail. Storm systems can move in quickly and unexpectantly, posing a potential threat.

Descend down the peak to the south on the South Loop Trail. The trail will follow the slope down into the Bristlecone pines. Continuing on the trail to the southeast, the trail will fork near Griffith Peak. Stay to the left and continue down into Kyle Canyon to complete the hike.

Fletcher Canyon

General Description: Diverse hike up a canyon to a stream.

Difficulty: Easy to spring, moderate up the canyon (rock scrambling)

Best Time of Year to hike: Spring through Fall

Length: 1.30 miles one-way to a stream, various up the canyon

Elevation: 6,925' at parking area, 7,975' at spring

Directions: Take US 95 north to the Route 157 turnoff. Travel west on Route 157. One half mile past the turnoff for route 158 there will be a turnout on the left for parking.

Hike: The trail-head is on the right side of the road. There is a forest service sign identifying the hike with a map of the area. Follow the obvious trail as it leads to the northwest up Fletcher canyon. This area has some very diverse vegetation; take note of the cactus and wild flowers in the area.

After 1.30 miles you will reach a small opening with a stream to your left. This is a good area for picnicking and for the less adventurous hiker, a good turn around point.

The trail from here becomes increasingly difficult with loose rock and rock scrambling. To continue on the hike, follow the trail directly across the stream or the trail to the northwest of the open area; they join almost immediately. From here the trail is much narrower, it follows along the left side of the stream, then through the stream for a short distance. Canyon walls become increasingly narrow. Continue on as far as you feel comfortable, then return the way you came.

Little Falls Spring

General Description: A short hike up to a small waterfall.
Difficulty: Easy
Best Time of Year to hike: Spring through Fall
Length: 0.35 mile one-way
Elevation: 7,645' at parking area to 8,435' at falls
Directions: Take US 95 north for 7.5 miles past Craig Road to the Route 157 turnoff. Travel west on Route 157 for 20 miles until you reach the parking area which is the first established parking area on your right after the extreme turn and ascent of highway 157.

Hike: The trail-head begins up the embankment at the parking area. Follow the trail to the right. Shortly after beginning the hike you will reach a fork in the trail, stay to the left following the trail as it leads uphill. The canyon will slowly close in, ending at small waterfall. Return the way you came.

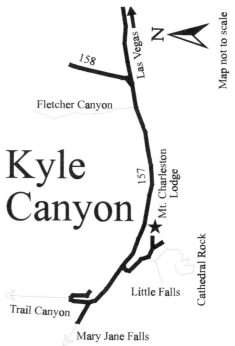

Mary Jane Falls

General Description: A mountain hike to a waterfall.

Difficulty: Moderate   (elevation gain)

Best Time of Year to hike: Spring through Fall

Length: 1.2 miles one way

Elevation: 8000' at trail-head to 8750' at falls

Directions: Take US 95 north for 7.5 miles past Craig Road to the Route 157 turnoff. Travel west on Route 157. Approximately two miles after the Ranger Station (which will be on your left) the road will make an extreme left turn. Instead, continue straight onto Echo Road. At the fork make a left onto a dirt road. Park at the dead end.

Hike: The trail is marked by information boards at the end of the parking area. The trail begins by gently winding up the canyon then it switchbacks up the mountain side. Be considerate, those hiking uphill have the right away so move to the side for them. The trail will become narrower and steeper as you near the falls. You will know you're close when you have a vertical rock wall on your right. The area with the falls is a great place to picnic. Return the way you came.

Muddy Springs

General Description: A really long drive for such a short hike, but the solitude and wild flowers make it worth it.
Difficulty: Easy
Best time of Year to Hike: Spring through Fall
Length: 1.50 mile round-trip
USGS maps: Charleston Peak, Cold Creek
Directions: Take US 95 north from Las Vegas to Cold Creek Road. After 9 miles make a left onto a dirt road. This road is not a good one, you at least need high clearance, possibly four-wheel drive. Always drive on the more obvious road, ignoring any roads that fork from the main road, this will lead you to the middle spring of the three Mud Springs. Follow this road for 6.0 miles until reaching a small open area. There is a small campsite on the right.

There is also a road that leads to the western most Mud Spring which can be distinguished between the middle Mud Spring by stock tanks in an open area.

Hike: This hike is more a really long drive with a little bit of walking but sometimes that's just what we need. It's also a great place for camping.

Hike up the dirt road to a fenced in area. This is the middle most spring of the three Mud Springs. By each of the springs you will see many beautiful wild flowers and wildlife tracks.

At the rear of the fenced area you will see a small trail going to the right and left. By hiking to the left you will reach the eastern most spring. At this spring there isn't very much water, but there is a prairie setting with green grass and wild flowers. The spring is about 0.25 mile away.

By hiking to the right you will reach the western most spring. Much more water flows here but more livestock frequent the area, so it tends to be muddier. The spring is approximately 0.5 mile away. In all cases, return the way you came.

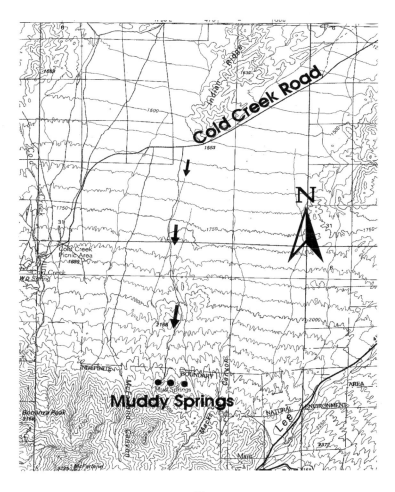

Mummy Springs

General Description: An interesting hike that leads through Bristlecone pines to a spring.

Difficulty: Moderate   (elevation change)

Best Time of Year to Hike: Spring through Fall

Length: 3.0 miles one-way from Route 158
   3.7 miles one-way from the Trail Canyon trail-head

Elevation: 7,620' at Trail Canyon trail-head, 9,483 at Mummy Springs

USGS maps: Charleston Peak and Angel Peak

Directions: This hike can be accomplished from two directions; the Trail Canyon trail-head or from the Route 158/North Loop Trail-head junction.

If taking the Trail Canyon route, take route 95 north to Route 157 (7.5 miles past Craig Road). Travel west on Route 157 for 20.4 miles until you reach an extreme turn in the road. Continue straight onto Echo Road until reaching extreme u-turn. Park on the left.

If taking the Route 158 / North Loop route, take Route 157 to Route 158. After passing the turnoff for the Hilltop Campground, park in the second pulloff on the left (4.8 miles from the 157 / 158 turnoff).

Hike: The Trail Canyon hike begins at the trail-head, then leads up the canyon. At the fork in the trail, hike to the right. There is a sign along the trail pointing the way to Mummy Springs.

If beginning at Route 158, hike west on the North Loop trail until reaching the turnoff to the right for Mummy Springs.

In either case return the way you came or if you have a car awaiting you, hike on the other section of the trail.

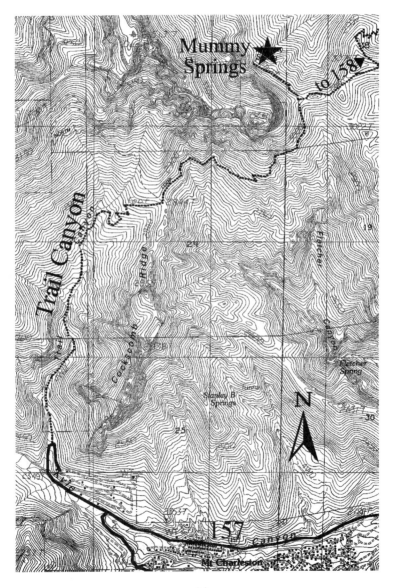

Robber's Roost

General Description: An interesting hike up a canyon to an old hideout for outlaws.

Difficulty: Easy

Best Time of Year to hike: Spring through Fall

Length: 0.5 mile loop

Directions: Take route 95 north to route 157. After 17.6 miles turn right on to Route 158. After 3.4 miles turn into the pullout on the right and park.

Hike: The trail begins across the road from the pullout. Follow the trail up the canyon. At the point where the caves become evident the trail is a little less distinct. The trail ends at the back of the canyon just past the caves. Follow the trail back out of the canyon hugging the right side of the canyon for the return leg of the loop trail or return the way you came.

The local folklore of the area is that outlaws used this area as a hideout due to its remoteness and the fact that you could see the law approaching from the high vantage point.

Trail Canyon

General Description: A pleasant canyon hike, or a way to access the North Loop Trail.

Difficulty: Moderate (some elevation gain)

Best Time of Year to hike: Spring through Fall

Length: 2 miles one way

Elevation: 7,615' at parking area to 9,335' at trail end

Directions: Take US 95 north turning west on Route 157. Continue on 157 for 20 miles until the road makes an extreme turn left. Instead of following the road to the left, drive straight onto Echo road. After 0.5 mile the road will make an extreme right, park there at the gravel area to your left.

Hike: The hike begins at a forest service sign designating the hike and providing information. The hike begins quite easily but quickly narrows and becomes steeper ending at a saddle area that junctions the North Loop Trail. Return the way you came.

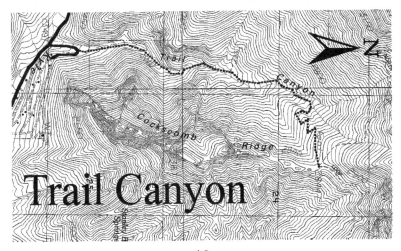

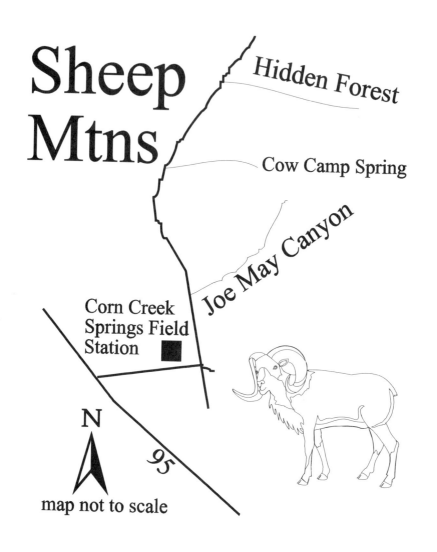

Sheep Mountains
Desert National Wildlife Range - Nevada

For more information:

Refuge Manager
Desert National Wildlife Range
1500 N. Decatur Blvd.
Las Vegas, NV 89108
(702) 646-3401

At the Corn Creek Field Station there are restrooms, information boards and pamphlets for the area.

Hidden Forest

General Description: This hike moves from open desert to mountainous pines.

Difficulty: Moderate   (length)

Best Time of Year to hike: Spring and Fall

Length: 5.0 miles to the cabin and spring

Elevation: From 5,800' to 8,000'

USGS maps: Black Hills, Corn Creek Springs, Hayford Peak, White Sage Flat

Directions: Head north on US 95 to Corn Creek Springs Road and make a right turn. There is a sign for the Desert National Wildlife Range indicating the turn. Drive until you reach the Corn Creek Field Station, then make a left turn just past the station onto Alamo road. Follow this road for 15.0 miles to the Hidden Forest turnoff to the right. From here the road becomes worse and high clearance preferably 4WD is recommended. After the right turn, drive for just over 3.5 miles to the end of the road/parking area.

Hike: Hike down a closed road into a large wash. The trail continues on this road up the wash. Eventually signs of the road will end and just a trail will remain. The vegetation changes significantly from desert to pines. Continue on the trail to the cabin. Near the cabin you would swear you were at Mt. Charleston with all the pine trees. A few feet before the cabin is a metal trough where the spring feeds. The spring's flow is often quite low so don't depend on it for a water source. Since this area is remote and cooler in temperature, it is possible to see a variety of wildlife. Return the way you came.

Joe May Canyon

General Description: A hike up to Whitehorse Pass
Difficulty: Moderate
Why: elevation change and length
Best Time of Year to hike: Spring and Fall
Length: 3.4 miles one way
Elevation: Beginning at 4740' at the parking area to 6860' at Whitehorse Pass
USGS maps: Black Hills, Corn Creek Springs
Directions: Head north on U.S. 95 to Corn Creek Springs Road and make a right turn (16 miles past Craig Road). At the Corn Creek Field Station make a left turn onto Alamo road. After three miles, turn east on Joe May Canyon road. Park at the "No Vehicles" sign on your left (after approximately 4 miles) which serves as the trail-head. The dirt road you have been driving on will continue, it leads to Little Joe May and Black Gate Canyon,

so watch carefully for the sign. If you drive past a corral, you have gone too far.

Hike: Hike down the closed road to the north east. The road is quite evident for most of the hike but if you lose it just continue up the large wash. After 1.5 miles there is a side canyon on your left (west) which leads to a man-made watering hole for the Bighorn Sheep of the area. Keep your eyes open, you might get a chance to see some sheep.

The last mile of the hike is the most interesting. You reach a grove of pinyon pine and juniper as the trail leads upward to a saddle called Wildhorse Pass. At the pass there are spectacular views of the area. Return the way you came.

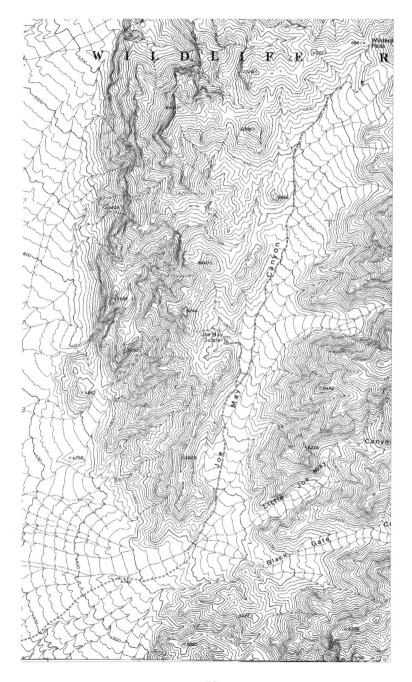

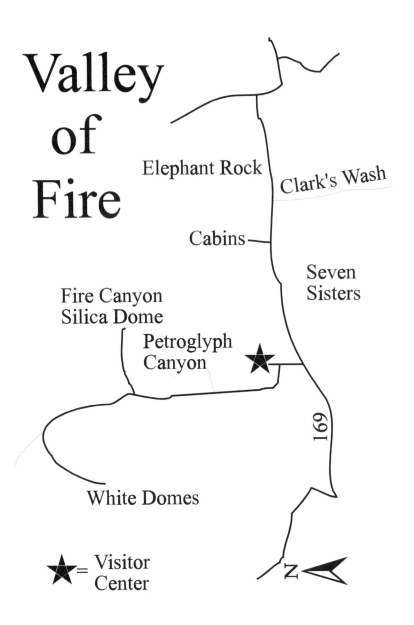

Valley of Fire

Managed by The Nevada Division of State Parks

For more information contact:

Valley of Fire State Park
P.O. Box 515
Overton, NV 89040
(702)397-2088

There is a fee to enter the park. Stop at designated areas for payment and a free map of the area.

Clark's Wash

General Description: A hike through a large wash to sandstone formations and to a desert spring.
Difficulty: Easy/Moderate (one area to climb down)
Best Time of Year to hike: Fall through Spring
Length: 2.5 miles one way
USGS map: Valley of Fire East
Directions: The hike begins off of Route 169 in the Valley of Fire State Park. It is east of the Visitor's Center and the Seven Sisters formation in a large wash which is marked as Clark's

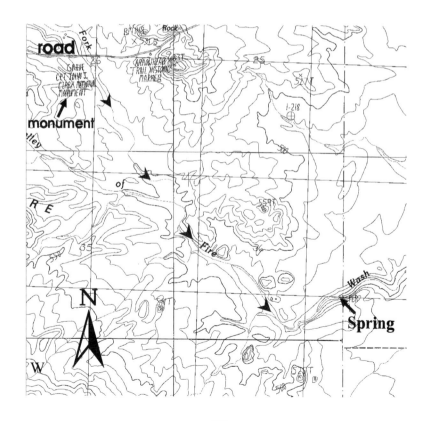

ash. Park off either side of the road.

Hike: The hike begins from the road south into the wash. Just into the hike you will see a large monument in reverence to Clark from hence this wash was named.

The first 2.0 miles of this hike are representative of a large desert wash. Just when you think you've had enough of trudging through the gravel of the wash bottom, the wash descends down through some beautiful red sandstone.

Around the corner water seepage begins and eventually a small stream begins to flow. Watch for wildlife that may be taking advantage of this precious water source. Return the way you came.

Petroglyph Canyon

General Description: A spectacular hike through a red sandstone canyon with petroglyphs, to Mouse's tank.
Difficulty: Easy
Best Time of Year to hike: Year-round
Length: 0.5 mile round-trip
Directions: Take Interstate 15 north for 22.5 miles past the Speedway exit to Route 169. Turn east on Route 169 and continue to the Valley of Fire State Park. In the park, turn left following the signs to the Visitor's Center. Just before reaching the center, the road will fork. Take the road to the left to the Petroglyph Canyon turnoff.

Hike: The trail-head is at the east end of the parking area near the restrooms. Follow the red sandstone as it curves through the canyon. Watch for petroglyphs on the canyon walls. An informative marker about the petroglyphs is near the restrooms. Remember that state and federal laws protect these drawings so enjoy the view but don't ruin them for others.

The trail curves to the left, ending at Mouse's tank. The tank is a natural depression in the sandstone which collects rain water. The tank was named for a Native American that used the canyon for a hideout in the late 1800's.

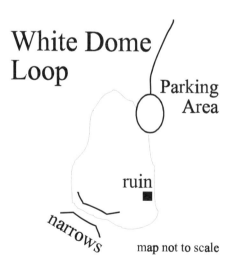

White Dome Loop

General Description: A diverse hike down to a narrow canyon and back out the other end to the parking area.

Difficulty: Easy/Moderate (some loose footing)

Best Time of Year to hike: Fall through Spring

Length: 1.0 mile loop

Directions: Take Interstate 15 north for 22.5 miles past the Speedway exit to Route 169. Turn east on Route 169 and continue to the Valley of Fire State Park. In the park, turn left following the signs to the Visitor's Center. Just before reaching the center, the road will fork. Take the road to the left. Follow the road past Petroglyph Canyon and Rainbow Vista. Follow the road as it curves around turning southernly to the White Domes parking area.

Hike: The trail-head starts from the end of the parking lot to the south. Hike down the hill to a building ruin made of rock (0.25 mile). Just down the hill from the ruin is a wash running northwest to southeast. Follow the wash to the right (northwest).

From here you will enter a short narrow canyon with high canyon walls (these canyons are so cool). After you exit the canyon head north along the trail. At the end of the trail you will pass between two sandstone mounds to reach the pavement. Then head towards the parking area.

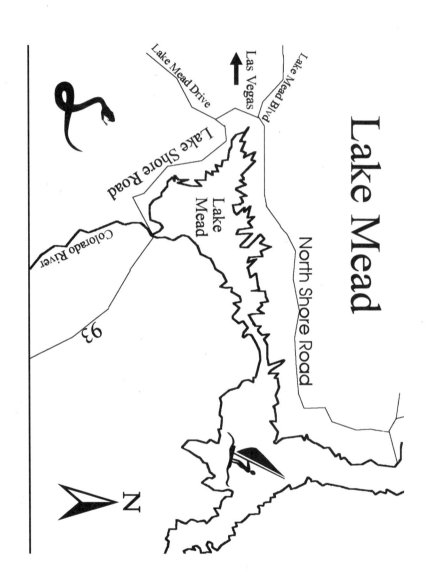

Lake Mead National Recreation Area

Managed by the National Park Service

For more information:

Alan Bible Visitor Center
(702) 293-8990
24 hr emergency number: (702)293-8932

A great way to see the Lake Mead area is by taking guided hikes from the rangers at the National Park Service. Hikes schedules are available for each season at the Alan Bible Visitor Center. The hikes are conducted on a weekly basis with a sign up system to reserve a spot on the hike. Pamphlets on trails in the Lake Mead area are available at the visitor center as well. Call the visitor's center for more information.

Bowl of Fire

General Description: A hike to red sandstone formations.
Difficulty: Moderate
Why: Last section of the hike is steep
Best Time of Year to hike: Fall through Spring
Length: 3.0 miles each way
Elevation: 1,969' to 2,264'
USGS map: Callville Bay
Directions: There are two ways to begin this hike; starting from Northshore Road at a pullout just past mile marker 18 or by following a dirt road that begins at milemarker 16. If you are starting the hike from Northshore Road, it will add 1.0 mile to your hike. From the pullout, hike across the desert. You will see the red sandstone formations in the distance. Hike towards the right of the formations towards a gray ridge with a saddle in front of the red formations. When you cross a large wash, look for a rock cairn indicating a road that leads up a wash. Taking the dirt road will lessen your hike by approximately one mile. This road is usually in good condition but it follows a wash and has soft, loose gravel which some vehicles may find difficult. Use your own judgement, but 4WD may be necessary. The road begins at the mile 16 marker, at the fork in the road, stay to the right. Follow the road keeping on the main path at all times. You will see a road off to your left marked by rock cairns. Turn to the left following the road as it winds around to the north and narrows slightly. Park at the sign marked "No vehicles beyond this point".

Hike: If you have chosen the dirt road begin your hike at the "No Vehicles" sign walking up the wash. If you have hiked from Northshore Road you will also find the sign.

The hike begins gradually as a wide wash with a soft gravel floor. This hike can be done in several different ways. First there are rock cairns that take you across ridges along the hike or you can follow the wash for easier hiking or you can just hike in the direction of the red sandstone and make up your own hike as you go.

If you choose the first two mentioned alternatives I would suggest taking a good look at the map in this book. At any rate what you are looking for is a section of red sandstone to the north. When you get close enough to see it, look at the left edge of sandstone. There will be a formation on the left, a small break and then more formations as you look to the right. You will be hiking around the left side of the sandstone, behind it and hiking up a drainage area to the open area in the formation. This gives a tremendous view of the area.

If you are following the cairns keep the formation in view and keep watch for the cairns. If you are hiking up the wash, the wash will become increasingly narrower. Unfortunately, following the larger wash for the hike will lead you to a different area which is actually quite beautiful too.

The trick is to branch off to the left at the appropriate place. As you are following the wash look for another wash joining the main wash at a 90° angle. On the left right before this wash will be a small number of trees. On the other side of the entrance to this wash is a large mound of dirt about 15 feet high.

From this point follow the trail up the wash. When you each the red formations follow the wash around the left side. Hike up behind it turning south when you see a large drainage. Hike up the hill. Return the way you came.

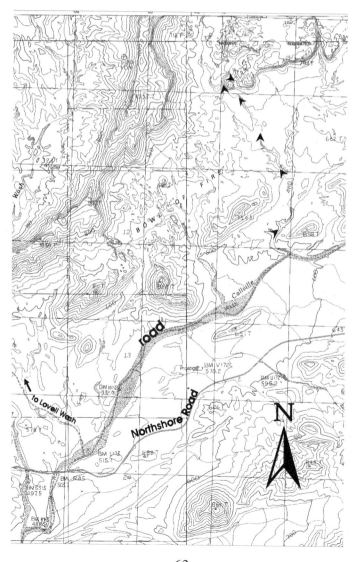

Callville Trail

General Description: A short hike to fantastic views of Lake Mead.

Difficulty: Easy

Best Time of Year to hike: Fall through spring

Length: 0.70 mile to various

Elevation: 200' elevation change

Directions: Just past mile marker 11 turn right, following the signs to Callville Bay. After several miles you will see a sign for the dump station. Park near the dump station either in the parking lot to the north or in the dirt lot to the south.

Hike: The trail-head begins on the north side of the dump station. Follow the trail approximately 0.3 mile until the trail forks. If you follow the trail to the left another 0.05 mile you will reach a hilltop which provides excellent views. If you follow the trail to the right you will pass a section of black volcanic rock. As you reach the top of a rounded hill the ground substrate will change to red and brown rounded rocks beneath your feet. This is another great viewing area. From here return to your vehicle, or continue on any of the other abundant trails in the area.

Gold Strike Canyon Hot Springs

General Description: A challenging hike down a steep canyon to a series of hot springs and eventually to the Colorado river.
Difficulty: Difficult (rock scrambling skills are necessary)
Best Time of Year to hike: Fall through Spring.
Length: 2 miles to the first hot spring
             4 miles to the Colorado river.
Elevation: 1500' at trail-head to 680' at the river
Directions: Traveling south on US 93, turn right 0.5 miles after the Gold Strike Casino. The turn off is not easily noticeable. At the turnoff you will see a sign designating the road as #75. Take this road until it separates into #75 (straight ahead) and #75A (to the left). Take #75A for approximately 1/4 mile until it dead ends. Park in the open dirt area.
Hike: The hike begins at the dead end, at a clearly marked trailhead. The trail begins pleasantly, with a wide trail curving through steep canyon walls. You will see a few wrecked vehicles and miscellaneous parts in various locations along the beginning of this hike, presumably from US 93 above.

The difficulty begins at about 1.3 miles into the hike with a sharp decent down a rock face. Steps have been cut into the rock making the maneuver manageable. Another 0.2 of a mile and you begin entering salt cedars, you may also begin seeing trickles of water here.

Throughout the hike there are arrows spray painted on rocks to identify the trail. Using these arrows can be quite useful if the next portion of the trail is not evident.

Just past 1.5 miles into the hike, there is a large drop off with a seemingly impossible decent. Move around the large boulders to the left, there is a trail that leads down. The hike becomes increasingly difficult from this point. There are sharp drop offs, small edges to traverse and even a rope to help you down some slick rock. Remember each move made down the canyon will have to be repeated for the exit back up. Know your limits and abilities well, this is a difficult and potentially dangerous hike.

As you hike down the canyon more water will occur until eventually you will be walking in water from time to time. Naturally occurring and man-made pools are evident at various locations throughout the decent.

Do not put your head under water, there is a parasite present in the water of the hot springs that can cause serious health effects.

To reduce the difficulty of this hike, enter the canyon by boat from the Colorado River, hiking up the canyon to reach the hot springs. Another alternative is to hike down the canyon and have someone pick you up by boat. Either way eliminates the strenuous climb out of the canyon.

Grapevine Canyon

General Description: A fascinating hike with abundant wildlife, vegetation and petroglyphs.

Difficulty: Easy to petroglyphs
　　　　　　　Moderate up the canyon (rock scrambling)

Best Time of Year to hike: Fall through Spring

Length: 0.4 mile to the petroglyphs, various along spring

Directions: Take 93/95 south out of town to the 95 turnoff just before Boulder City. Drive south for 55 miles until reaching the 163 turnoff to Laughlin. Head east. Turn left after approximately 14 miles onto a dirt road. After about two miles turn left again, the road dead ends at the parking area for Grapevine Canyon.

Hike: The hike begins at the end of the parking area. Follow an obvious path paralleling a large wash on your right. After 0.40 mile large rock formations mark the entrance to Grapevine Canyon. Take note of the abundant petroglyphs etched into the boulders.

　　　Hiking up the canyon, you will reach the runoff from a spring in the canyon. Following the spring further up the canyon is exciting, but the hike becomes more difficult with rock scrambling a necessity.

　　　This spring provides much limited water to the desert attracting all types of wildlife. Watch for the Chuckwalla; a desert lizard. They are commonly 10 inches long and have a stocky appearance with a greyish to black coloring. Also take note of the vegetation like the canyon grape growing along the spring.

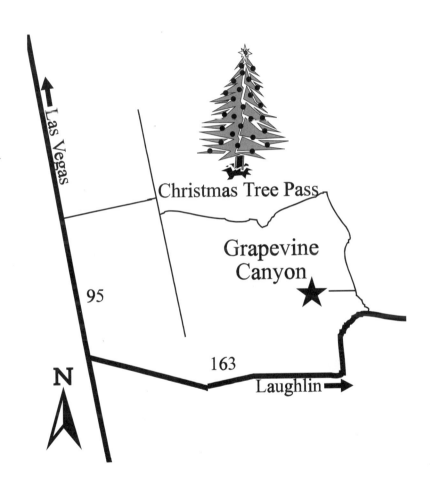

Historic Railroad Trail

General Description: An easy hike along the railroad line used to build Hoover Dam in the 1930's.

Difficulty: Easy (flat and easy terrain-good for bikes)

Best Time of Year to hike: Fall through Spring

Length: 1.3 miles one-way

Directions: Take 93/95 south out of town to Boulder City, at the stoplight make a left following 93 toward the Hoover Dam. Turn left onto Lakeshore Road towards the Alan Bible Visitor Center. Make the second right (the first is to the visitor center) into a parking lot. The trail-head is off the south-east end of the parking lot.

Hike: Take the trail to the east as it follows the path the historic railroad used to bring equipment to construct Hoover Dam. Construction began in 1931. The railroad was in use until 1962. This hike will lead you through a series of four tunnels. The fifth tunnel was sealed in 1978, and is the end of the hike. Throughout the hike there are spectacular views of Lake Mead on your left. Return the way you came.

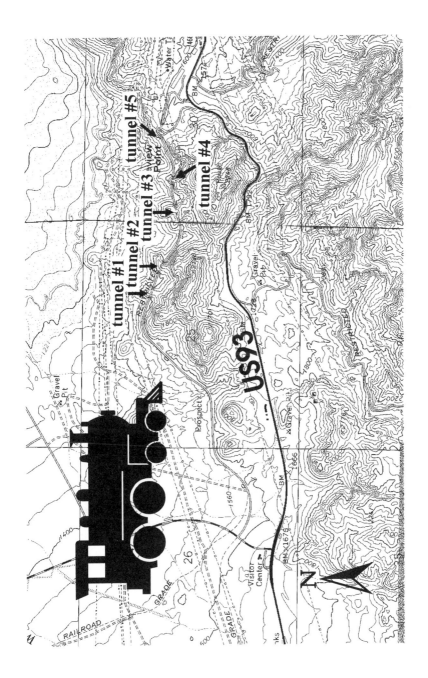

Horsethief Canyon

General Description: A hike up a desert canyon to a waterfall.
Difficulty: Moderate (elevation change, some steep hills)
Best Time of Year to hike: Fall through Spring
Length: 1.5 miles one way
Directions: Take U.S. 93 south across Hoover Dam to the Arizona side of the river. Between mile marker four and five there will be a short dirt road with a parking area on your right. Drive just past the parking area to a dirt road on your left. Follow the road over an old bridge. There will be a road to the right just past the bridge as you drive up a hill. The turn is very sharp, and has a sign for Horsethief Canyon. Take this road. From here the road becomes questionable in some areas requiring the use of at least a high clearance and probably a 4WD vehicle. It is four to five miles to the parking area and trail-head.

Hike: Begin the hike at the dry waterfall at the parking area. For those adventurous in nature, climb up the waterfall (the right side is easier). For those more skeptical, hike to the left of the waterfall up the hillside and then downslope to the wash above the waterfall.

Follow the main wash as it twists and turns throughout the canyon. There are a few spots of rock scrambling if one is so inclined but it is not necessary as alternate routes are abundant. Dependant on the time of year, water is available through about half of the hike in the form of a small stream. Wildlife use this water daily so be on the lookout, especially for Big Horn Sheep. There may be a spot or two where you question what direction to take. At one point you reach an area where straight ahead is a smaller wash with a steep incline, instead follow the main wash to the right, it will shortly meander back to the left and will dead end into a box canyon type of area with a large waterfall. Don't expect large volumes of water to be draining down the falls, it is dependant on the time of year, but a trickle of water is probably more realistic. There are large cottonwoods in this area which makes for a great picnic spot. Return the way you came.

The story of this canyon is a fellow stole a horse in Kingman and rode up the canyon being chased by a band of men. He rode up Horsethief Canyon only to be boxed in at the waterfall area. He was apprehended and apparently hung on the cottonwoods. But as the Park Ranger explained to me, those cottonwoods would not have been tall enough to hang a man that long ago. So whatever the truth may be, it still makes a good story.

Lovell Wash

General Description: A day hike in a wash past a mine to a narrow wash with high canyon walls.

Difficulty: Easy (small amount of rock scrambling)

Best Time of Year to hike: Fall through spring.

Length: 1 mile one way.

Directions: Take Lake Mead Boulevard east over Sunrise Mountain to the stop sign. Turn left onto Northshore Road. Make another left onto a dirt road at mile marker 16. The parking for the trail-head is 1.85 miles down this dirt road.

This road is not suitable for all vehicles, a high clearance vehicle is suggested and possibly 4WD, dependant on the road conditions. Continue until you reach a fork in the road. Keep to the left. After just over a mile you will see a large sign on your left. The parking area is another 0.6 mile. Park on the left or right where the road slopes down into a very large wash. You will see two red hills on the far side of the wash.

Hike: Begin the hike down the dirt road into the wash. Turn right and hike up the wash. At this point the wash is very wide. You will see several old mines on both the left and right side of the wash. These are remnants of the Anniversary Mine (1922-1928) which mined for calcium borate. This area is popular with rock hobbyists.

As you follow the wash, it will abruptly become very narrow. This area is spectacular with high canyon walls and water etched stone. This narrow area is often very cool providing pleasant relief from the heat. There are a few areas where minimal rock scrambling is necessary to continue up the wash.

When you reach the end of the narrows you will have hiked about a mile from your parked vehicle. Keep on the lookout for bighorn sheep, they are often seen in this area. Return the way you came.

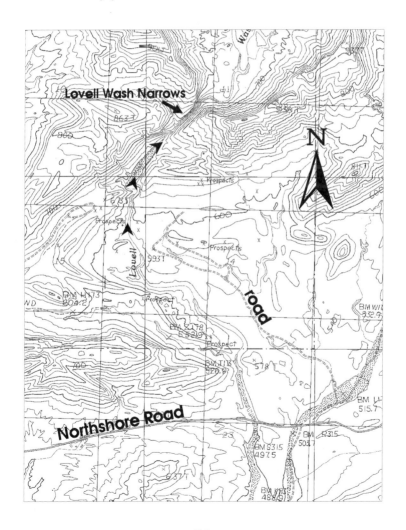

Northshore Summit Trail

General Description: A short hike to spectacular views of red sandstone mountains.

Difficulty: Easy (elevation gain, watch drop offs!)

Best Time of Year to hike: Fall through Spring

Length: 0.25 mile one-way

Elevation: 200' elevation change

Directions: Take Lake Mead Boulevard east over Sunrise Mountain. At the stop sign make a left onto Northshore Scenic Drive. Make a left into the parking area just past mile marker 20. The trail-head begins at the parking area.

Hike: Follow the trail up the hillside. At 0.25 mile you will reach a saddle among two hilltops. This saddle provides remarkable views of the neighboring mountains and valleys. The red formation is called Bowl of Fire. Hiking to the right up a narrow trail about 0.1 mile will provide a slightly higher vantage point.

Redstone Trail

General Description: A fun and informational loop through sculpted red sandstone formations

Difficulty: Easy

Best Time of Year to hike: Fall through Spring

Length: 0.5 mile loop

Directions: Take Lake Mead Boulevard east over Sunrise Mountain. At the stop sign make a left onto Northshore Scenic Drive. Make a right at mile-marker 27 into the Redstone Picnic Area.

Hike: Begin the hike from the east side of the parking area. You will see an obvious path. All along the path are informative plaques educating the reader on the formations and geology of the area. The path winds around to the right bringing you back to the parking area.

River Mountain Trail

General Description: A trail leading to a series of mountain top overlooks.

Difficulty: Moderate (elevation gain)

Best Time of Year to hike: Fall through Spring

Length: 2.0-2.6 miles one-way dependent on overlook trail

Elevation: 2400' to 3500'

Directions: Take 93 south to Boulder City. Follow 93 as it turns left at the stop light in Boulder City down towards the lake. The trail-head is on the left, 0.6 mile from the stoplight. At the turn there is a sign indicating the trail, and a small bridge over a culvert. Park in the designated parking area. The trail-head begins at the information board.

Hike: At the sign post area there are informational pamphlets about the hike. Sometimes there are none available, so get yours next time you visit the Alan Bible Visitor Center. The pamphlet contains a map of the trail and an informational guide that corresponds to marked areas on the trail. At each designated sight the pamphlet informs the hiker about the immediate area. This is a great addition to the hike and worth the extra effort of getting a copy.

The hike begins gradually at the information board in the parking area. The first portion of the hike is a gradual incline, from there it goes into switchbacks with a greater elevation change. After 2.0 miles the trail forks on a ridge line.

This can be the end of your hike or from here one can continue to the right to the Black Mountain Trail (0.6 mile) and the Bootleg Wash Trail (0.6 mile) or to the left to the Red Mountain Trail (0.3 mile). See the map for more insight.

I prefer the Black Mountain Trail because it gives a spectacular view of Lake Mead.

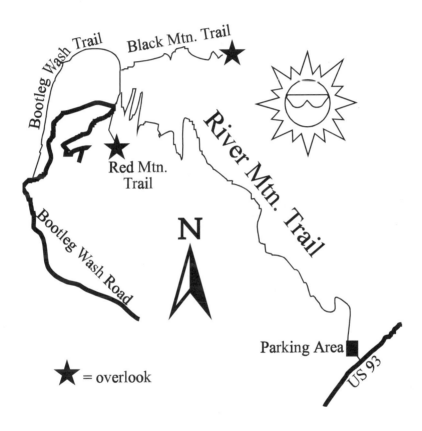

Roger's Spring Trail

General Description: Two hikes are possible here; a gentle ascent to an overlook of Lake Mead or a level walk along a stream bed.

Difficulty: Easy

Best Time of Year to hike: Fall through Spring

Length: various

Directions: Take Northshore Road from Lake Mead Blvd. (over Sunrise Mountain) to mile 40, park in the parking area on the left.

Hike: If you are pressed for time this is a great way to view both an overlook and a desert stream without much walking. The hike begins at the parking area, move along the east (left) side of the pool formed by the spring for approximately twenty feet. You can hike to the right to the scenic overlook, or to the left along the stream. There are several areas to cross over the stream if you're interested. Habitats such as these provide shelter and food for many desert creatures.

Wetlands Trail

General Description: A loop trail to the Las Vegas Wash
Difficulty: Easy
Best Time of Year to hike: Fall through Spring
Length: 0.75 mile loop
Elevation: 100' elevation change
Directions: Take 93/95 south to Lake Mead Drive in Henderson. Turn left following Lake Mead to the Northshore Scenic Drive turnoff to the left. Just past the bridge over Las Vegas Wash you will see a parking lot to the right. The trailhead begins from the parking area.
Hike: The hike begins near the portable toilet facility in the parking lot. You can follow either part of the loop first. The left or northern most route descends into and follows a wash down to the water of Las Vegas wash. The right or southern most route follows a ridge-top down to the water where it meets the other leg of the trail. The Las Vegas Wash runs through Las Vegas and is a tributary to Lake Mead.

The foliage along the banks of the wash are primarily Salt Cedar also known as Tamarisk. This plant stabilizes the banks of the wash and provides habitat for birds of the area.

White Rock Canyon

General Description: A hike down a large wash to the Colorado River at Ringbolt Rapids with a side trip to hot springs.

Difficulty: Moderate to Colorado River
Moderate/Difficult to the hot springs (rock scrambling)

Best Time of Year to hike: Fall through Spring

Length: 2.5 miles to the Colorado River
another 0.5 mile or more to the hot springs

Elevation: 1600' at the parking area to 680' at the river

USGS map: Ringbolt Rapids

Directions: Take U.S. 93 south across Hoover Dam to the Arizona side of the river. Between mile marker four and five there will be a short dirt road with a parking area on your right. Park in the parking area.

Hike: The trail-head begins at the parking area. Follow the beginning of the trail as it parallels a large wash. Drop down into the wash and follow it to the river. The wash will widen and narrow repeatedly throughout the hike, with a long stretch of high canyon walls.

From the river, walk left (south) to the hot springs and ascend up the next side canyon. The hot springs form a series of pools. Continue as far as you wish but remember access to the pools becomes more difficult as you ascend up the canyon. Return the way you came, the elevation gain will make the return trip more strenuous.

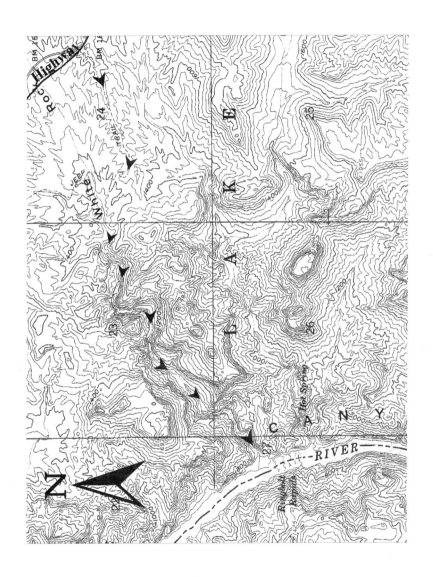

Keyhole Canyon

General Description: A very short canyon hike with petroglyphs to a dry waterfall.

Difficulty: Easy

Best Time of Year to hike: Fall through spring

Length: 0.15 mile one-way

Directions: Take the U.S. 95 turnoff near Railroad Pass south. Six miles past the junction of NV highway 165 (16 miles from 93/95) turn onto a dirt road to the left. Continue on that road for 2.1 miles under a set of power lines to the second set, turning right on the power line road heading south. After 1.8 miles turn on a small road to your left which will lead you to the parking area for Keyhole Canyon after 0.3 mile. These roads are not suitable for all vehicles so take caution. A high clearance vehicle is recommended.

Hike: The hike is really too short to even be called a hike but the petroglyphs and dry waterfall make the area interesting for a picnic or a camp out to get away from the hustle and bustle of Las Vegas.

Enter Keyhole Canyon from the parking area through a fence. Follow the canyon back to the dry waterfall. The majority of petroglyphs are at the mouth of the canyon. This is also a popular rock climbing area so you may see some climbers in action.

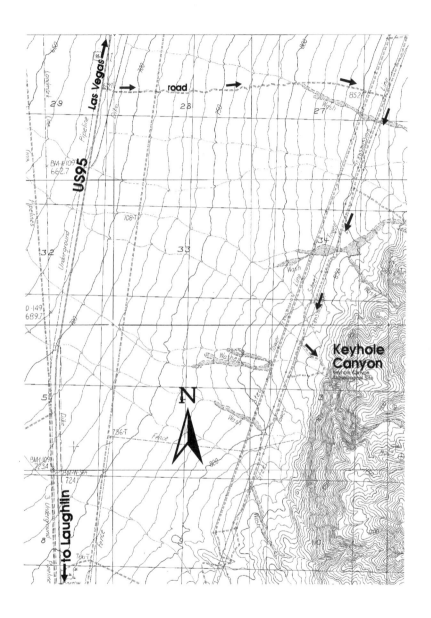

THE TOP 10 HIKES

#	Hike	Difficulty	Why it's a favorite
1	**Lost Creek**	Easy	Diversity (open desert, stream, vegetation and rock formations)
2	**Lovell**	Easy/Moderate	I love slot canyons!
3	**Redstone**	Easy	Great picnic area, cool sandstone formations
4	**Grapevine**	Easy/Moderate	Petroglyphs
5	**Goldstrike**	Difficult	Hot springs, the Co. River and lots of scrambing
6	**Turtlehead**	Difficult	360° views
7	**Ice Box**	Moderate	rock scrambling
8	**Railroad Trail**	Easy	tunnels and great views of Lake Mead
9	**Petroglyph Canyon**	Easy	Petroglyphs and sandstone
10	**Cathedral Rock**	Moderate	spectacular views

Parents with Children

Several hikes in this book are wonderful for children. The terrain is easy, there are interests for the children and the danger level is low, making it less stressful to take them with you. Here are a few:

Children's Discovery Trail Informative and fun (see description for the workbook that accompanies the hike)
Lost Creek short, diverse
Moenkopi near Visitor's Center, short, hilly
White Rock Spring a short walk down a hill to a water basin
Little Falls Spring short hike to a waterfall
Petroglyph Canyon terrain is easy, watch kids climbing on rocks
Grapevine to petroglyphs, further up canyon is more difficult
Historic Railroad Trail very flat, wide and easy but the sides drop down sharply, also good for bikes
Redstone very fun with information boards throughout the hike but watch kids playing on sandstone, it can be dangerous.
Keyhole Canyon petroglyphs at the mouth of the canyon and a short walk to the waterfall (usually dry), hazard is kids climbing on rocks.

A couple of these hikes would be very scary with an exuberant youngster. If there is two it might not be so bad, but if you are outnumbered I suggest you don't undertake the following hikes:

Keystone Thrust big drop-off at the end, can be avoided
Cathedral Rock the area with the views has serious drop-offs
Northshore Summit again, serious drop off at the view point

And any of the hikes that have rock scrambling, unless parental help is easily accessible to the child.

SPECIAL THANKS

I would like to thank Linda Lane for giving me the confidence and guidance to attempt such a project. My husband; Bill and mother; Sylvia who went on many of these hikes with me, along with various friends and family who did the same. And my father; George for helping me fit hiking into some of our weekend outings.